Mystical and Kung fu-ey

Aparna Rao

BookLeaf Publishing

India | USA | UK

Mystical and Kung fu-ey © 2024 Aparna Rao

All rights reserved.

No part of this publication may be reproduced, stored in a retrieval system, or transmitted, in any form or by any means, electronic, mechanical, photocopying, recording or otherwise, without the prior written permission of the presenters.

Aparna Rao asserts the moral right to be identified as the author of this work.

Presentation by *BookLeaf Publishing*

Web: www.bookleafpub.com

E-mail: info@bookleafpub.com

ISBN: 9789363308923

First edition 2024

*To my daughter Shraavyaa and husband
Subbu—you are the reason I fly but also why I
stay grounded. Thank you for teaching me how
to love.*

Sunday and Monday

He feels like a Sunday,
Light, relaxed and something you look forward
to…

My husband feels like a Sunday,
While I am probably a Monday.

We couldn't be further apart.

He is the relaxed brunch of pancakes and dosas
and mimosas;
I am the hurried morsel you put into your mouth
as you rush out the door.

He reminds me of oil baths and afternoon naps
and Netflix movies,
I am the whirlwind Monday—trying to catch
your breath as you pray for it to be over so that
you can go home.

Sunday and Monday. That will never work they
say…

Little do they know Monday gets through the
week rushing past every deadline so that it can
meet Sunday.

And Sunday brings a smile to Monday's face,
where she can finally rest her head on his
shoulder before the morning rush again.

Home

They tell me my approach is unhealthy
When I say I feel I don't belong; that nothing
feels like home anymore.
I feel I am transiting, but now I have had enough
of the transit, it's time to go home.

I know I have a purpose and it's not time yet, but
how do I make myself at home.

And what is home?
Is it where I was born—I don't feel connected,
Is it where I grew up—I don't live there
anymore and have faint memories.
Is it where I got support and started fresh?

The yearning for afterlife doesn't go away.
I remember, I remember the bliss that I don't get
here.
How can I be happy when everything here is
temporary, it's like staying in a hotel.
How do I explain the yearning and longing? To
whom do I explain?

I have never fit in. Not as a child.
They spoke to me because I was the smart kid
with glasses whose notes they could
borrow—but I was different.
I never understood conversations and still don't,
heck at times I felt something was wrong with
me.
I was too sensitive, no wait, over-sensitive was
what my class teacher had told my parents.

Not as an adult.
When I hear them brag about their countries,
their food—I am glad they are so proud but I
don't understand it.

You are in one country today, and you could be
born in another tomorrow. So what? This is not
your home.

I don't say this—I don't want to be ridiculed.

My daughter when she was 5 used to say 'Hosa
mane!!!' or 'New home' every time we entered
a New hotel room during our travels.

I found that very refreshing.
Maybe because I have changed so many houses
in my lifetime.

But underneath everything I just cannot shake
the feeling that everything, everything is
temporary.

But if everything is temporary why do I feel the
need to belong here then?
Am I missing something?

It's only after decades of exploring I realize. I
belong. In myself. To myself. And the body may
change, may grow older and I may change it
altogether in another life. But I belong to the
soul. I am the soul. And at last, I realize my
folly. I am my own home.

Surrender

The need to be the best.
Followed me, drove me
For every exam or test

It led me to make work my all
And at times I couldn't hear anyone else call
The best at work, the best at home, the best in
my hobbies, the best everyday
Until one day I stopped and said—hey!

Why am I competing with my child at ludo
What did I expect that she'd say—Mama kudos?

Today as I look back I see
And life teaches you the hard way—gee
Winning is not possible in everything
And at last, I soften, slow down and think

The only way to win at something is to actually
surrender to it completely.

Daughter

Those big eyes on her little face
Make me gasp at their beauty when she opens
her eyes after an afternoon nap.

I can see the whole universe in them
Shiny, sparkling caramel-coloured jewels

Look at me with the love of lifetimes
Like I can do no wrong
As her tiny blush lips smile and she almost lets
out a little chuckle

How can my heart be in the tiny fist of a
nine-month-old

It's as if I haven't ever known love before and
will not now know anything like this again

Her soft hazelnut wisps of hair gently falling on
her forehead with the breeze.

She cuddles and snuggles to me and I give her a
light embrace.

Is this what love is, this maybe heaven.
And I want to be stuck in this moment forever.

Food for Gods

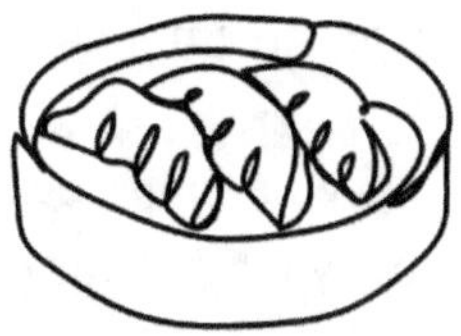

The first sleepy sip of ginger tea in the morning jolting all your senses awake.

The soft melt-in-your-mouth idli with the pure coconut chutney, the fragrant coriander one or the spicy tomato chutney

The crisp dosa with the piping hot sambhar, the more decadent Sister–the Davangere benne dose with the bland potato filling but heavily spiced dry coconut chutney and a dollop of butter to make up for it. Or the ghee drenched mulbagal dose when you want to challenge your heart.

The crisp crunchy vada with a soft inside.

The hot malpuas sipped in decadent sugar syrup and then with the rich creamy rabri.

Dark chocolate. Just being dark chocolate. The darker the better.

Warm, comforting gulab jamuns, little balls of
deep-fried dough in sticky sugar syrup matched
with cold vanilla ice cream.

Hot chocolate on a cold night, every sip making
your throat and body a little warmer with each
slurp.

Onions bhajjis, ridge gourd or capsicum pakoras
on a rainy day, the spicy savory gram-floured
chili snack leaving you wanting more.

The smell of coffee anytime anywhere awakens
a distant long forgotten memory.

The cheesy goodness and stretch in a freshly
made pizza.

Tomato and basil soup with a dash of pepper
with gooey grilled cheese.

Avocado goodness on toast with a dash of lime
and some chilli and cilantro.

Spicy, sweet, salty, tangy tamarind rice or
poha/avalakki with freshly grated coconut.

A bar of Twix shared with my daughter.

30 seconds in the microwave and eating it
dripping with ghee, the loveliness that is Mysore
pak.

Fresh decoction in my filter coffee.

A scoop of homemade, fresh off the stove kesari
bath to lift your mood with extra ghee and sugar.

The coconut jaggery elaichi combination in
Indian Sweets.

Corner house ice creams.

My late mother-in-law's rasam. And gojju.

My mom's vegetable korma.

The first mouthful of panipuri with spicy and
sweet chutney in just the right proportion
bursting with flavor.

Never-ending pavs to go with your
finger-licking lemon squeezed onion added
bhaji.

Hot fried kunafa with gooey cheese in sugar
syrup and a scoop of Nutella.

Chocolate cake from Magnolia.

Brownies from Theobroma.

Aloo parathas, the heavenly spicy potato-filled
rotis with cold yogurt and pickle.

Chai after every meal, chai at breaks, chai
anytime. The dark cinnamon coloured elixir
warming up every pore in my body giving me
hope and strength to get through the day.

Kaju katli. Ten of them at a time.
What do you think of when you are fasting?

Grief

It comes unannounced.

Sometimes, when I am at work.
At times a face at the airport reminds me of
them.

Occasionally, it's a word or a dialogue on TV
that takes me back.

And then there's a flood of memories. Of
images.

The softness of her cheeks, her red round bindi,
the oil from her hair slowly flowing to her
forehead.

Her simplicity, her glass bangles.
Her infinite patience.

Always pushing us to do better and better. Her world revolving around her children. Cooking everything from scratch. Her experimenting with different cuisines.

I remember her sarees, her very long hair. Her love for gardening.

How do you get over the loss of your mother?
I mean, she's the one who's always there.
She's the rock, you always know she's there for you,
the strength and support behind the scenes.

She's the one to turn to when I am feeling sick,
when I have a question about my child, when I need a recipe, when I have to vent.
And she was a doctor, so all the more reason to ask her a million questions.

If I would get home from college and she wasn't there, it would bother me.
Whom do I look to now?
What does one do without their mom?
You always need your mom no matter how old you are. And the one time I need her more than anything, she's not here…

Divine

That first glance, the familiarity; I knew.
My eyes seek you out in a crowd,
You became my refuge, my home.
My heart listening to words unspoken, unsaid.

I knew the sound of your footsteps
I could sense your arrival despite the crowd
My mind constantly at war with my heart
Trying to balance doubt with belief

Your one glance could take away my pain
Your divine countenance fills my eyes
Whose heart is filled with divine love,
How can worries enter that place?

In the midst of daily anxiety and chaos,
You became my guiding light
Guiding my every step, lifting and inspiring me
Regardless of the storms I face

Prayers, meditation, rituals are a thing of the
past,
As I feel your presence intertwined with mine.
My soul is set free by your name
As I walk my path in your grace.

I trust in you as I seek my way
And your name to brighten my day.

Spirituality

A million thoughts in my head as I close my day
Tired and weary when I decide to get back home
I can't hear the words of my soul anymore
I seem to have forgotten who I am.

Daily hustle. Annoying drama. The little jiggling
thought that stays in my head from the day
Small inconveniences that won't matter in a few
days.

I get back home with my mind a mess
A little furry tail wagging uncontrollably greets
me.
Close behind is my little girl so happy to see me
A call or text from my husband checking if I got
home chimes

The daily chores and work angst do quiet down
Like someone turned down the volume

After a cuppa with my daughter, I freshen up.

I am calm but I need to wipe off the dust on my
soul like the—new dish scrub of greasy dishes.

I need to remind myself of the deeper truth that
guides me like a shining light.

Meditation. The reminder of beyond this realm.
Stillness. Reflection. Quiet.

I can hear my soul whispering to me,
I can hear the echoes of the divine,

I find the answers to my questions,
My soul finally starts to shine
The connection to the divine grows a little
stronger just like the network bars on my phone

I talk to God like He's my friend.
I believe He can hear me and I can Him
I have always done that all my life
The fear-driven or the prayers for asking for
things never resonated with me
The conversation with a friend lifts me up again

I embrace my journey once more
I let the soul steer and guide me
In this quiet place, I find myself again
I trust the guidance, my voice
And once again I feel truly whole.

Perseverance

There's something about not giving up. In spite
of what everyone tells you

They mean well. This isn't worth it, it is hard,
Maybe something else will be more suitable?

There's power in carrying on, something almost
divine

The is a glow radiating from those who hang on
unwavering and strong.

Through all the obstacle and challenges faced
Perseverance triumphs; washing away all the
pain

One day at a time, with faith and hope on our
side
Pushing through each problem, never giving up

We are destined to win, bringing light to the
darkness.

And showing everyone how it's done.

Love

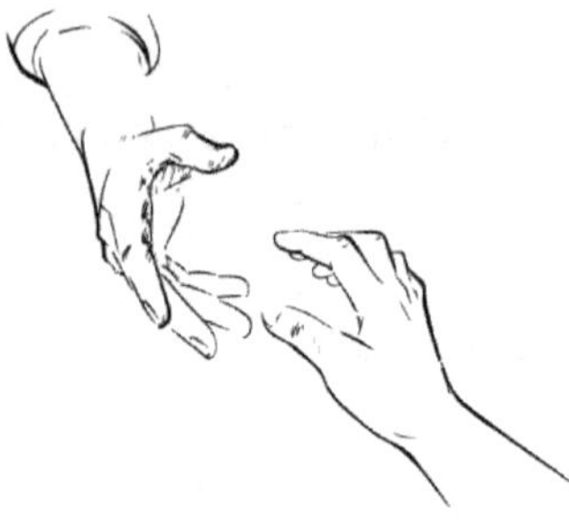

A peek of sunlight on a cloudy day
A single lone flower facing the sun in the whole
bush

A smile, a call to check up on you
Offering you the last piece of cake

Driving a few hours to get your favorite thing

Being at your side through the worst tragedies.
Silent. Strong.

The first call to tell you good news.
Tons of laughter.

Singing about you at random times, catching
you by surprise

Love defies logic, it transcends reality

It believes in you more than you believe yourself

Filling hearts with divinity,
A concept beyond understanding

A force, a power, a mystery, an energy
The strength to bind hearts, minds and also souls
in its grasp

Magic. No poem or book can capture.
Everything stands still in its experience

Boundless, miraculous, blessing, gift
Soaring, levitating, traveling beyond realms.

Forever binding. Forever intertwined.

Self Love

Dear Body, I am sorry!

I have hated you forever.
Compared you to many,
Didn't embrace you for who you are…
Didn't cherish your light and shine.

You tell a thousand tales
Every wrinkle, every stretch mark, every bruise.

I wish I treated you better
With gentle care,
Nurturing every pore,every hair
You are, after all, my house in this lifetime.

I spent millions on my house and style
So much on my car and what fuel went into it
But I wronged you
With the wrong fuel and also pushed you with
no respite.

I didn't focus on your strength or your charm
Didn't set your spirit free or soothe you.

Now as I turn forty-five I hope you forgive me
A little late but I start the journey to love you
right.

Looking at you makes me smile,
I celebrate the beauty that you are,
How did you put up with me all these years
You are a wonder, and my pride.

I hope you feel safe to shine your inner self
As I learn to embrace the joy of caring for you.

Addiction

Liquid or powder maybe
Some get high with a puff or a whiff

Mine is disguised as hardcover or paperback
Words on paper weaving magic
A portal to another world.

Each book, a different world
Giving flight to my thoughts
Echoes of different lands and times
In perfect symphony and rhyme

Companions, teachers, and hope givers
Dare I say, good friends
Each book telling a different tale
Oh how I mourn the turning of the last page

Guiding me through life's ways
Thank you rustling pages for holding me in your
sway.

Unconditional Love

Eyes wide and trusting, happiness unmatched,
The love you shower upon me when I walk in
that door,

Snuggling up for a cozy cuddle,
Hearts so forgiving and forgetting the past
Loyal and playful you protect my home

Boundless energy, radiant smiles
Chasing balls and barking at birds

Furry bundle of joy, lighting up my soul
Warming up my hearts and igniting spirits

Lucky are those who experience a love like this
Know what it is to feel eternal, everlasting and
divine bliss

The more I meet people everyday I ponder
Why can't we be more like our furry friends I
wonder

Happy with small things, greeting everyone with
love
Loyal to a fault, always forgiving
Seeking the sun and taking many naps
Always hungry and ready for a walk.

Journey

All of forty-five I look back at my life
It's been a simple life full of joy and pain

Love, family, friends, ambition, grief, holidays,
changes, kindness by the universe

Gratitude fills my heart for the abundance I have
seen. Rich bonds, kind friends and a lot of love.

I look ahead wondering what's next

No big plans, ambitions or goals,
Just a desire to nurture my soul,
To find solace in the ordinary,
And embrace life's beauty.

This humble life, I want to share
With the people I love and care,

In the end, I seek no wealth or fame,
Not to win the lottery or some game
Just to have touched a few with a light flame
Maybe someone will look back at my name

She left behind a life well-lived,
A legacy of love and kindness to her name.

Dad

A hard life full of struggle
A self-made man who only knew troubles
He worked hard and then some more
But every time he lost more than he could make

Highly educated, no task was beneath him
Only wanted his children to be independent
You never know how life turns out—he said
Don't depend on others, fight yourself.

Several illnesses plagued him
But his steady presence was strong and true
A father's love was there to be felt
He didn't express it or share it very well
But everything he did is etched in my mind

I wish you could see us now and know
Though time has passed your legacy lives on,
In the values you've instilled, the lessons you
taught
Your quiet love, will always be treasured
And cherished always, beyond measure.

All or nothing

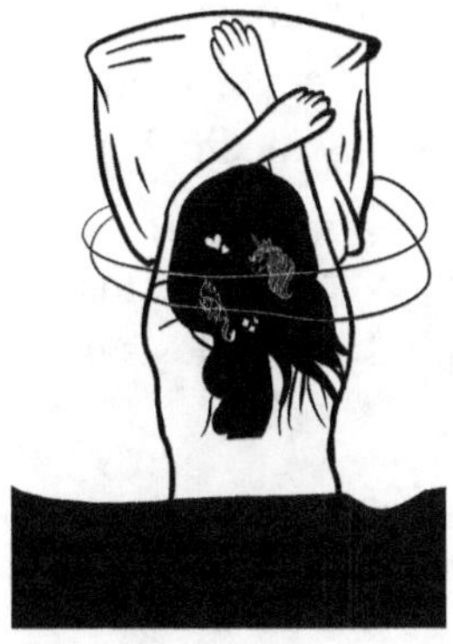

I have always been extreme
Love something or hate it, no in-between

Be balanced I am told.
Do everything in moderation.

I don't know how.

Fiercely protective of my loved ones
Loving them to the point of obsession
What's the point if it doesn't consume you
entirely?

Moderation is boring, moderation doesn't excite
me. I cannot fathom it.

Food, music, art, dance, love, work, hobbies…
the ecstasy of losing myself to my passions and
letting flow through my very being...
Transporting me to another world.
It's my worship, my meditation

Halfsies have never been for me
I care or I don't. It's simple as that.

Sounds

Rafi's voice, honey flowing
A melody begins to flow.
It's soft and sweet, almost like spell,
Makes me feel comforted like a hug

Sufi melodies pure and strong
Transported to another realm
A timeless dance, a scared soulful flight,
Through the whirl, my heart ignites.

Devotional songs, echoes of a mystical call,
In every rise and gentle fall.
The yearning for the creator through the strings
and beats
In God's hymns, my heart's retreat.

I wander through the voices
Rafi's, Sufi and bhajans
A world of love, of joy, of pain,
In every word, breath and note, I live again.

In these moments, soft, quiet and deep,
The songs of old, my soul they keep.
They lift me up, they set me free,
In each note and lyric, eternity.

A symphony of stars dancing above,
A testament to God's endless love.
In Sufi whispers, I find myself whole,
As Rafi's voice bandages and heals my soul.

So let tonight embrace this orchestra,
Where past, present and future intertwine.
There is only now, there is only this moment
In the divine harmony, I'm gently curled,
By this blessing, to another world.

Old is good

I woke up this morning, my joints creaking
Each step I took my feet took a beating
With wrinkles mapping out my eyes
I gasp—is this how it's going be till I die?

My hair, once dark and luscious, now fairly
gray,
Reminding me constantly that my youth is
slipping away.

I bent to tie my shoes today,
And my belly came in the way

I move my books or phone far away
To read texts and what it has to say
Labels on food in tiny sizes
I wish life had a real-time zoom function

My memory is being a comedian
Thinks it's the main actor in a stand-up
I take a walk and then call for back-up
Search for my phone night and day
To find them in the fridge, no way!

Groans, grunts and sighing away
Mark most of the music of my days

Yet through moments of feeling older
A certain freedom and getting bolder
With every year the wisdom grows
One learns to enjoy the highs and lows
And not to mention the aches and woes

Cherishing each moment however small
Finding the beauty in it all

This journey is full of lessons learned
loving the sunshine, the rain and storms.

Sisterhood

I have been always told
A woman is a woman's biggest enemy

Then why is that every time it's a sister who's
come to my rescue out of the many

In the intricacies of my life, sometimes bland
and mostly grand,
The echoes of sisterhood I understand.
From childhood, college days to work, many
paths we've had,
In every moment, I have been held by an
invisible sacred bond.

To my sister, my rock, my strength,
With you, my mind and heart will always have a
friend
With you, I can share anything—my triumphs
and my fears,
Not worrying if this bind will withstand the
years.

In laughter and tears, in my brightest and darkest
hours
Your presence, your love, your guidance
Has always been around me.

I have found sisters and families in friends and
colleagues too,

Walking tighter, hand on hand
With our hair flying in life's shifting breeze

Through shared glee and woes
Through every challenge, every care
You had my back when things were bleak
And danced with me at the peak

To all the sisters in my life,
Who stand with me through everything,
Hand in hand, we find our way,
Together, come what may.

Far and wide

In the rains of Seattle and the hustle of New
York

The arch of St Louis and the winds of Chicago,

The museums of Washington DC,
The universities of Boston
The mountains of Costa Rica
From America's shores to Argentina's tango,
I've wandered the world, finding each place.

In France, I strolled through sunny streets,
In Wales, I saw the castles and the Celtic greets.

Lake District's charm, lavender field, smitten by
England's charm,
Scotland's highlands, a majestic land.
In the Netherlands, cheese, canals and tulip
fields,
Belgium's chocolate and TinTin!

Germany's tales of castles and friends,
Spain's La Ramblas, a vibrant scene.
Rome's history and Venice's beauty
Switzerland's peaks, where the mountains thrive.

Poland's cities, Czech's Prague,
Hungary's Budapest, a jewel so bright,
UAE's deserts and endless moonlight.

Kuwait's nostalgia, Bali's water sports
Singapore's gardens, Thailand's temples,
Maldives' islands, a wonderland.

Kashmir's beauty, Amritsar's divinity
Kerala waters, Vizag's caves
In each of these places, I have traveled far and
wide

From continent to continent, sea to sea,
Each journey, a treasure, a cherished memory.
With every step, I have searched for you, every
flight a story to tell,

Of all the world's beauty, there hasn't been a
person like you. Unmatched, unique and just
right.

Thanks my dear husband, for being the soothing
balm to my anxiety,
The laughter in the mundane days
The comfort during anguishing days
The bright sun rays peeking out of clouds on
dull rainy days.

It's ok to choose yourself

I open the paper
Who wore it better, it says? Pitting two actresses
against each other.
I turn the page. The "other woman" is blamed
for seducing a married man.

I put down the paper and take a walk
Women, frantically getting their children ready
for the day balancing lunch boxes, yelling at the
bus driver to wait.

I remember my anxious moments as I used to
get my daughter ready for school.

Anxiety, hurry, worry, work, panic, tears, getting
it all done.

The strongest thing in the world is graphene they
say. I think it may be a woman's heart.

It holds the weight of the world's expectations,
Unfair comparisons, shaming and name calling,
The dreams of parents, hopes of self, so-called
"honor" of society,
Love of husband, the pain of their children,
The responsibilities of home, the aspirations at
work,
The patience for relatives, the neglect of self, the
cruelty of loved ones, the kindness of friends,
The hope for change, the faith to move
mountains,
The strength of a saint, the burdens of ancestors,
the bias of managers, the underestimation and
judgements, the betrayals of trusted friends, the
labels…so many labels.

And yet she gets up the next day and gets back
to being strong.

I wish someone tells her that it is ok.
You don't have to be strong.
Your don't have to carry the weight of
everything on your shoulders.

Put that boulder down. You are not perfect and
that's ok.

You don't have to please anyone.
You cannot and don't have to make anyone
happy.

You can stop the cycle. You can be…you.
You can choose yourself. And that's ok.

Signs

The day after my mom died
I woke up as normal and made two cups of
tea—for the both of us
Only to wake up to the reality that she's gone.

Loss. Having something one day and it
disappearing the next leaves a hole in your heart.

You fill it with sugar or fries or other distraction
but it doesn't work.

I ask for a sign that she's around.
A sky-blue elephant I say.
I feel stupid when I say so.

Days pass and the world seems to be moving
along just fine.
Somehow oblivious to the loss I feel.

A friend invited me home after years
It's always nice to be amongst friends

He shows me his new house.
I enter the kids' room and stop in my tracks

Goosebumps. I forget to breathe.
The entire wall is painted with a sky-blue
elephant.
And his son is playing with a plush toy.
An elephant. Sky-blue.

I breathe again. I look up to the heavens, eyes
filled with overflowing flow.

Thank you. Thank you. Thank you.

Generation to generation

Every parent does the best they can,
Not just raising their children;
But also growing up with the child.

Unintentionally traumatizing the child
And pass on their unresolved issues

I look back with understanding and sympathy
now,
Because they were also born with me;
First-time parents.

As I grow up with my daughter now,
I think I am doing the best…
But thoughts cross my mind time and again…
What am I passing down to her?
In spite of the best of intentions

My anxiety, my worry, my sense of dread
The knots in my stomach before every big
event?
My anger, my guilt, my pain…
How can I sieve out the unwanted?
And only pass on my wit, my smile, my
compassion?

Will she blame me when she grows up?
Will she think she got the raw end of the deal?

How can I make her only the best of me?
And is the best of me enough…

I don't know the answers and I may never know
But I can love her the best I know each day

Rest

In a world full of hustle and bustle,
Everyone running and cars honking,

People walking really fast like they are doing
something very important.

I want to rest.
Close my eyes and look at the clear blue sky;
Warm days of sunshine on my face.
Feeling the grass beneath me,
Listening to the birds chirping

Listening to my breath.

And once again I have a little bit of life in me
To join the hustlers and the bustlers

To push through another day.

Heartbreak

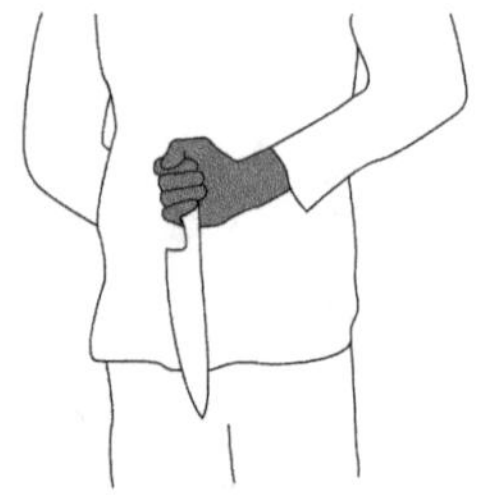

I listen to songs.
Most are about love.

The melancholic songs are the best.

The lyrics, the melody is just haunting

But I cannot find the right one to match my vibe
today.

Your heart doesn't break only in love;
Friendships break your heart too.

A betrayal far deeper at times.
I chose someone as a friend…
And shared my life with them.

Laughter, food, drinks and sharing of hopes,
dreams and pain.

Friends to strangers, the pain is real,
But I don't have a song to cry to…

Silently I weep for the time gone by,
I miss you my friend, but I don't want you near
me anymore.

Letting go

There's a strange thing I notice about myself
The more people say I can't do it, the more I do
it..

There's an inexplicable feeling in doing things
that presumably cannot be done.

But I don't know when to stop.
I don't and can't let go.

Like the Venus fly trap killing itself on the chilli;
I hold on to things far longer than I need to…

Illusion

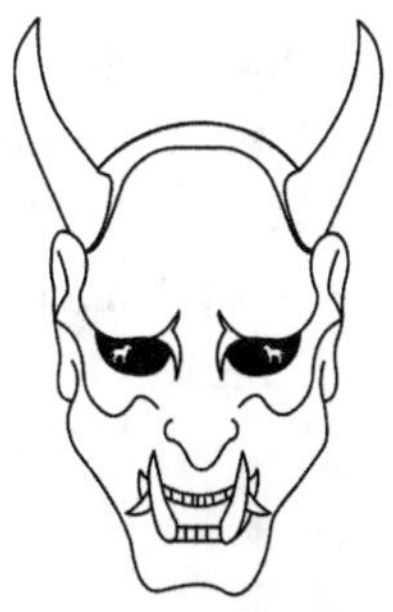

What's the point of this human life?
If it's spiritual attainment and nirvana;
Why do we spend all our energy
In taking care of our bodies,
When we should be taking care of our souls?

Our souls move on to the next life
Our bodies don't.

I don't know what to make out of it—
Chasing behind money,
Chasing behind the shiniest gadgets,
The holiday abroad,
Playing dirty at work,
Being unkind to one another.

I wonder what the person above is thinking
As they are shaking the snow globe from time to
time and looking at us all play our roles…

Doing everything against our true nature,
Straying farthest from our paths,
Do they laugh or do they sigh?
Shaking their head with utter disbelief

Do they think—the most dangerous creation of
mine is the human being?

Unfinished

Do you ever look back…
At places, friendships or jobs?

Unfinished business,
Incomplete canvases,
Movies without an ending,
Incomplete symphonies,
Unwritten chapters,
Inconclusive episodes,
Unfulfilled promises,
Unaccomplished dreams,
Half-done buildings…

Maybe that's why ghosts exist
Hauntings need not be only in spirit.

My inner child

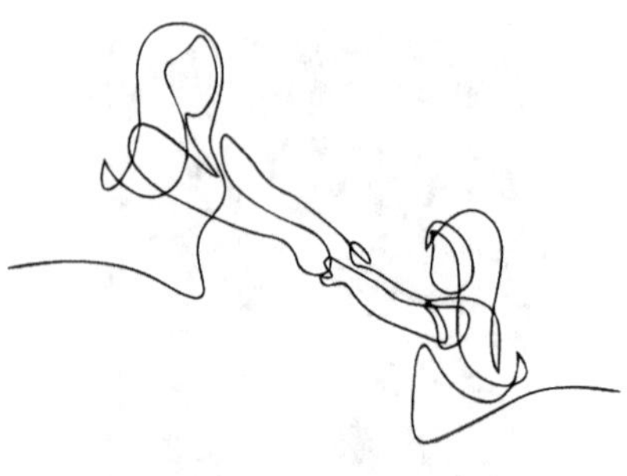

I wish I could travel back in time and speak to
the little me
Sitting side by side
Looking at the little one with two pigtails
Chubby and wide-eyed

It's ok
It will be ok
You are enough
You have always been enough
Your sensitivity is a strength
Your kindness is a superpower

You will love many things in life but learn to
love yourself first
It's ok to put yourself first

Always, always, always trust your gut, it never
is wrong
If someone doesn't treat you like the absolute
amazing person you are, don't let them into your
life.

The right people will come.
Your tribe will be amazing.

Petals in concrete

Staying soft in a hard world; by choice

Not letting the roughness touch my spirit
The thorns not able to get to my inner bloom

Bruised but not broken, keeping my heart
unhardened even though I am surrounded by
harsh forces

An unarmored heart has its own charm.
You can sense it a mile away
It acts like a lantern in the dark.

My garden of gentleness, precious, strong,
unaffected by the world,
the wildflower it is…

One can't crush a sponge.
Its softness and permeability is its strength

Absorbing all the energy around it
Soaking every moment, every emotion

Holding all the joy and laughter
Wringing out all the negativity

Cleansing itself over and over

Empty nest

I know it's coming
No more homework
No more school books and uniforms strewn
around

No more PTM meetings and school events
No more chaotic sharing of the day's events
Before stringing off to the next activity

The hugs, the fights, the calls to pick up from a
place
The piling up of clothes for a certain theme at
school
With the constant "I have nothing good to wear"

No more "Borrowing" my T-shirts and jewelry
Finding my deo in your room
My eyeliner at your table

No more "I want to eat ___________ "
No more yelling at you to go to sleep early

I waited for the chaos and busyness to end
And now that it's coming close…

I would give anything to extend it by one more
day.

Defiance

There's a certain kind of peace
When you accomplish things that are assumed
impossible

There's a certain kind of power
When you don't let others define you

There's a certain kind of joy
In putting people in their place when they
underestimate you.

For someone who loves words, it's ironic
I choose actions to shut people up.

Quietly. But surely.

Feelings

I have always felt. Everything.
Deeply. And thought it's a curse

I cry for those who are hurt
I cry for those who hurt
And I cry for me

I cry when I read the news
I stopped reading the news or watching TV

I don't want to feel this pain.

But without feeling
I am not me
You are not you

And we are alone

Feeling everything,
deep pain and unimaginable joy
Is what makes us, us.

Toddlers

Pitter patter of tiny feet
Unbalanced wobbly gait
Skin like butter, soft and smooth
Naughty giggles marked by high-pitched shrieks
in between

Faster than the road runner
Quite a feat to catch up
The unbridled joy in everything
Playing with everything within hand's distance

Unfiltered, unmasked and untouched
Filling the entire room with light
Such radiance that you want to wake them up
when they sleep
The house is silent without the music of their
anklets

What a gift children are
Tiny little humans
Filling our lives with such exquisite joy
And leaving us better 'cause of their presence.

Blessed

The voice within me
The knowing
The feeling

That I am divinely protected
Guided and anchored

Watched over

The more I stay true to myself
The more I hear my inner voice
The path shows up in front of me

Nudging me ahead.
Held by an invisible hand
Taking the next step with me

I never go wrong when I listen to the knowing
But sometimes my head takes over
This doesn't make any sense, it says

Be practical, be logical…. why would you take
this decision?

It's easy to ignore the quiet voice
In the daily grind and fast-forward speed
But it's there, quietly knocking till I listen

And when I am brave enough to trust it and
surrender
The magic happens
And I sit back and watch in wonder
At the path unfolding

The magic is me
The divine in me
If I let it win.

Tomorrow

Why is that tomorrow feels more hopeful than
today?

Why do we look at tomorrow like it will be
dramatically different than today?

Tomorrow smells like hope and a fresh start
Of miracles big and small
Of possibilities and change…

Yesterday is looked at with fondness
Nostalgic and precious, the moment gone by
We try so hard to save yesterday, through
photographs, videos and journals
Through mental snapshots and conversations

Yesterday fades away slowly and painfully
From our grips like water trickling away

It's almost like today has no value
With our hearts stuck in yesterday and minds
focused on tomorrow

We know that today was also a tomorrow full of
hope…
and will become a yesterday looked back on
with longing

Yet today gets the short end of the stick
Everyday. Over and over again

Stuck in this endless loop, in its own Groundhog
Day

Funerals

There's something reassuring about a funeral
Reminding you that you are also on borrowed
time
That this is all an illusion and your true place is
somewhere else

To make the most of the time left
To enjoy every moment
Funerals give you a sense of detachment

Two weeks after a loved one passes
Is something special indescribable

You recollect every moment with friends and
family
You look back with so much fondness
You celebrate the life of the passed one
Cry your heart out and say your goodbyes

You resign yourself to the fact that they are gone
Not fully comprehending it yet, the grief hasn't
hit you, it comes much later

When you are alone and doing something you
enjoy.

It hits you out of nowhere and paralyzes you.
Life is never going to be the same again

But you don't feel that at the funeral. Not yet.
It's more a chance to honor the departed
And you get together with family picking apart
every photo, every shared moment, reminiscing
their quirks and sharing stories

There's something special about that
You don't do that ever again

Grief at a later date is something very personal.
The uninvited guest
The dark cloud over your head
And you can't detach any more
The family and friends are gone.

You are alone. With your grief.

Things that make me think of you

Long car rides. Filter coffee.
Walks. Dad jokes. Bad jokes
Loud laughter. Innocence. Simplicity.
Teddy bear. Pillow. Strength.
Humor. Gold. Pillar. Sugar
Warm sunny mornings.
Pleasant evenings
Friendship. Marriage.
Calm. Peace. Home.

Boundaries

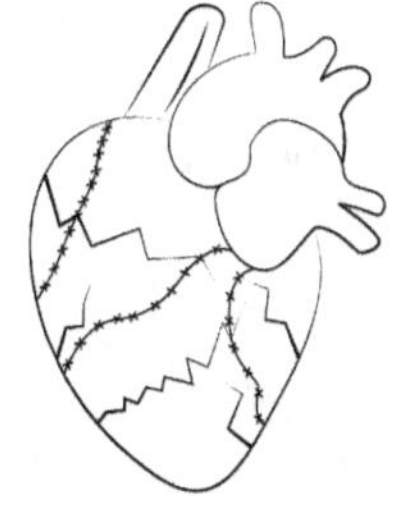

I gave and gave.
I thought I was doing a good thing.
After all, what's life if not in service of others?

Until I gave too much.
I had nothing left.
I was empty.

And yet the asking never stopped.
The taking continued until I said—enough!!!

That was the biggest lesson of my life.
To know when to say—enough!

Now I give.
But to myself. And if I have something left.
To those who deserve it.
And not to those who ask or take. Or need or
want.

Those who still cared when I was empty, those
who protected me from coming down crashing
Those who tried to fill the void with their
presence.
Those are the ones who deserve.

Countries

I sometimes imagine countries as humans.

America as a chubby, donut-eating, hustling
busy, blond man.

France as a petite,young lass in a white sundress
eating a croissant.

Iceland as a green-eyed handsome loner with
dark secrets.

Argentina as a couple, one a raven-haired tango
dancer with a footballer, full of life and energy.

Italy as a romantic, twinkling-eyed tall man.

Switzerland as a blonde woman with beautiful
blue eyes.

London as a learned, poem-churning bookworm.

China as an overachieving, can do it all woman.

Germany as a scientist who doesn't like to be
disturbed.

Would I be friends with them?
What would happen if these personas were in a
room for a meeting? Would they fall in love?

Would they have adventures together?

I wonder if I will ever know as I wake up from
my nap.

Right moment

A moment too long…
The chai bubbling out of the vessel onto the
stove,
The pancake burning on the pan,
Missing the stop on the bus,

A moment too long…
The biscuit falling into my cup of chai,
The toast hitting the ground jam-side down
gathering all of Scooby's hair,
The ice cream melting all over my hand,

A moment too long….
Missing the subway,
The gates closed at the airport,
The cab driver no longer there,

A moment too long…
The climax of the latest thriller dragged into
absurdity,
The teams call with the round table,
The project supposed to be over the last quarter,

A moment too long.
Regret.

But the moments too soon? Longing

A moment too soon
Playing fetch with Scooby
Laughter and lunches with friends
My daughter's childhood, her screaming "Amma
" in glee whenever she did something herself,
and wanted to proudly show me…
The time with my parents
Meeting my siblings in other countries
My youth
My energy
The excitement when I try something new…

The right moment, the right length of time.
Elusive.

Silence and solitude

My time alone. I guard like snakes guard
treasure

Loneliness you may call it
I call it my pleasure

Quiet, unintruded, my happy place
Gathering my thoughts, going at my pace

I dream, I think, I draw, I sing
In my kingdom, I am the kind

My imagination takes flight
I fight to protect it with all my might

How do you come up with such great ideas?
They ask
I smile to myself…I can only truly unleash my
inner self when I don't wear a mask

I find peace in myself
Not in a place, person or thing
People come and go, seasons change and things
are temporary

My solitude is mine and only mine.

Giving up

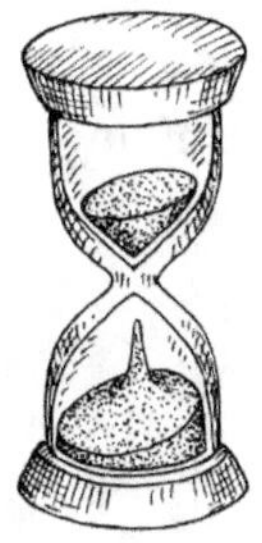

When should one give up?

When the very thing you are holding onto starts
eating you from the inside

A job or a situation or people

When is the right time to leave?

When it begins to change you more than you can
contribute to it

People ask you—why are you leaving, you are
doing great?

You smile to yourself. Is this what I want to do?
Is this where I want to be?

I can't explain. I want to. I cannot get the right
words

This isn't mine anymore. My place is elsewhere.
My heart can feel the promise of a better
tomorrow.

She

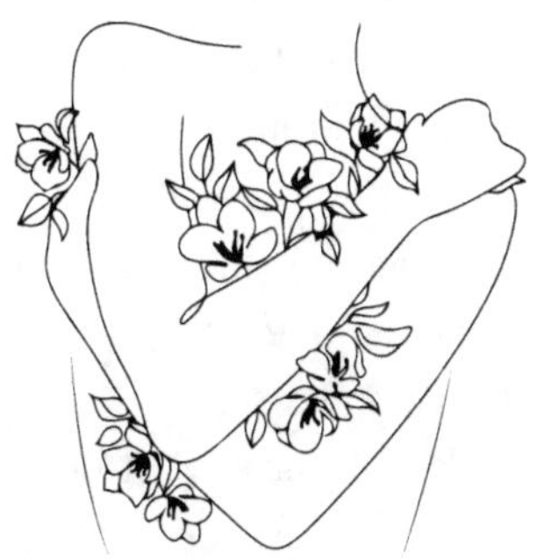

She's a child of the Gods bathed in divinity
Don't mistake her for weak

Her smile may mislead you
Her tears make you misjudge her
She can burn your whole world to pieces if she
chooses to

She's kind, she's tough, she's rare
And she will make her soul bare
She can let go of things not serving her, without
a care…

She doesn't want small talk and superficial
conversations
She will go deep if you hold her hand
She will run through your veins and consume
every thought

She's the movie with twists and turns that make
you laugh and then cry with intensity
She's the book you can't put down
The song you hear on repeat

She's the name you blurt in your sleep
The drink you are addicted to
The rose you save and also
The poetry book that you save it in

You are lucky if you come across her
Don't be fooled by the gentle smile
She's the hurricane you thought was a breeze.

Fading Images

The person who walked me from school and got
me an ice cream when I was a child

The stranger who helped lift my daughter's
buggy down the stairs.

The stranger you sat next to on a flight and
realized she grew up in Salmiyah, Kuwait too.

The panipuri wala who asks you why you didn't
come for so many days, the cab driver who
shares his story with you.

The neighbor girl who you played every evening
with, now just a memory.

The first-grade teacher who built your
confidence.

The classmate who you met everyday before
school started because you both reached early.

The classmates who walked back home with you

The college professor who took the whole class
for a movie.

The tuck shop guy who made hot kachoris
everyday which we devoured after college

The colleague's dabba you finished in the office

People whose names I may not know or
remember.
Yet from time to time I think of them and
smile…

Passion

Have you loved something so much that it
completely takes over you?

Every minute every second you are consumed
by the thought

Images etched in your mind's eye

The first thought when you wake up
Constantly at the back of your mind

The last thought you have as you waft off to
sleep
The dreams every night

Everything around you constantly reminds you
of them

Love comes in all forms
But the ecstasy is losing yourself in it

Completely immersing yourself, surrendering to
it, to the point that there is no difference between
you and love

You become love. Love becomes you.

Little things

It's the little things

The opening of windows when I wake up, the fresh breeze hitting my face.

The sun rays warming up a cold day

Chai. Anytime. Anywhere

The flavor of mint in the middle of the day, waking you up

The smell of coffee wafting through the halls

Tomato soup on a chilly night

Cold lemon juice on a hot sunny scorching afternoon

Someone checking on you if you have reached;
or

If you have eaten

The reassuring smile when you most need it

The playful look your way

The eye contact

The hug when you most need it

Little walks around the neighbourhood

Your daughter snuggling up to have sneaked into
your bed in the middle of the night

Rainy days

Afternoon naps

Warm blankets.

It's always the little things.

Cut

It's ok to cut people off
That aren't good for you
Slowly sucking your energy
Bit by bit; you feel like a shell of yourself
Friends, family, acquaintances

I am told—No, that's not how society works
Aren't you spiritual? Shouldn't you accept the
good with the bad?
Be practical—what if you need them someday?
They are meant to be that way

I used to be called Mother India
Almost as if I have to carry the weight of the
world like she did

But I don't want to be a martyr

And so I cut people off

Sometimes you have to cut off the infested plant
so the rest grows

And it's ok.

Sunshine

Some people are the color yellow
Sunshine in human form

One conversation with them lifts you up
They move from person to person igniting their
light
Long forgotten
Rusted by the daily mayhem of life

Warmth, radiance, humor and energy
Rays literally sprouting off them

Who lights them up I wonder
Where do they recharge from
I don't know the answer
But I watch them in awe

Sharing their gift. Generous and limitless

Games

What a terrible irony it is
When you chase after something it just runs
faster

When you stop, it comes closer to you
Jobs, people, money, even spiritual attainment

I wonder if the Almighty is running a version of
games and watching from afar

Will they now pause and understand?
Or continue to chase?
Why don't they realize…
What's meant for them will come to them but
only when they don't need it anymore…

Letter to my daughter

Dear Daughter,

Have you taken a moment to realize just how amazing you are?
My heart swells with pride as I watch your achievements unfold before my eyes. All of sixteen trying to take over the world.

You always hold true to your values and refuse to settle for anything less than what piques your interest.
It's amazing how you stay true to yourself and inspire others along the way.
 I truly wish I had your strength and conviction when I was your age.

If only you could see yourself through my eyes, my love. You are this beautiful, adorable girl, determined to leave her mark on the world.
You have no idea how incredibly proud I am to call you my daughter.

Remember, it's not just about the outcome or
what you achieve, it's about who you are at your
core that fills my heart with immeasurable joy.

You have accomplished so much already, but
this is just the beginning, my dear.
 I am excited to see where your journey leads
you, and I will be by your side, cheering you on
every step of the way.

Life has its way of testing us, but always
remember that you possess an incredible
strength within you.
In times of doubt or despair, look within
yourself, for you will find resilience, courage,
and a spirit that can withstand any storm.
Surround yourself with those who uplift and
support you, and never hesitate to lean on their
shoulders when you need to.

I know life can feel overwhelming at times,
babydoll. The weight of endless expectations
can burden your dreams and tire your spirit.
But remember, my love, that you were born to
shine. Embrace your passions, chase your
dreams with unwavering determination, and
never let anyone or anything dim the brightness
of your soul.

The world is not always kind.
There will be people you meet who will not
always want the best for you.
In fact, may actively try and bring you down.
But there will also be people who will love and
care for you.
Choose wisely.

Don't let self-doubt hold you back. You are
enough. You can do anything you want. You
CAN change the world.

You don't have to be perfect
You don't have to be the best at everything
You just have to be you…

I always want you to remember that I am here,
waiting for you.
You are my greatest achievement, my pride, and
my eternal love.
I will forever be your advocate, your confidante,
and your unwavering supporter.
Please carry my love in your heart, let it
empower you, and let it remind you that you are
never alone.

With all the love and pride in the world,

Amma

Overachievers unite

You don't have to be the best in everything.
I read that again.
And again.

The anxious overachiever in me needed to see it.
And show it to my daughter as well.

I push themselves to the point of overwork
In an effort to achieve impossible standards.

And validation.
I am often told—wow, you are a superwoman.
Was sent an image of a woman with multiple
arms multitasking
With laptop in one hand and book in another
With a spatula in one and a baby in another

What am I trying to achieve
Whom am I trying to please
Whose standards am I trying to live up to?

I don't want to be a superwoman
Or a martyr
Or an overachiever
Or an angel

I want to be happy
Enjoying what I do.
Stopping something if I don't feel like it

I will not try to be the best. In everything I
touch.
But just a little better than yesterday.

Beauty of imperfection

Some days I am unstoppable
Wake up ready to conquer the world.
Other days the bed is my safe haven
Getting up feels like an uphill task.

Some mornings, I kill it—5 miles walk, crush
my presentation, and a chapter written before
lunch.
Other days, I struggle to eat without spilling all
over,
Am I getting old, I start to question

And that's okay.

Embracing the highs and lows,
Recognizing that every day is a new chance to
grow.

No judgments, no expectations,
Just acceptance and self-love, in every way.

For in the beauty of imperfection, I find myself,
my voice and my strength.
A reminder that I'm doing my best, and that's
enough. That's ok.

Contradictions

A multitude of contractions I am
Tangled multicolored threads

Planned but also spontaneous
I crave solitude. I like to be invited too
(I may not show up though)

Intuitive and emotional but also logical and
practical,
Confident but full of self-doubt
Strong they all say, but open and vulnerable.

Hate parties and gatherings and too many people
Love spending time in small groups
A stable adventurer, an extroverted introvert
An optimistic skeptic, a high-strung dreamer

Hate the spotlight but love to be on stage
performing…
Rebellious but also conforming, cautious but a
free spirit.
Creative perfectionist full of ideas but cautious

Puzzling to myself, a paradox at times
Finally embracing my mess and beauty
A work in progress drifting through life.

The Gentle Revolution

Kindness, compassion, love,
liberating and softening hearts,
Uniting us in quiet strength,
a gentle revolution starts.

Let us rise with empathy and grace,
Igniting our hearts,
Embracing our shared space.

Come together, for we shall
Listen more deeply, judge less often
Heal our wounds and soothe the broken
Choose words that uplift, heal and inspire
Nurture a world where love never tires

The Gentle Revolution begins within,
A quiet uprising of heart and mind.

Join the movement, be the change,
Let kindness foster and create a new tomorrow.

www.ingramcontent.com/pod-product-compliance
Lightning Source LLC
LaVergne TN
LVHW050912200726
843508LV00011B/2185